Books by Adele Faber and Elaine Mazlish

Between Brothers and Sisters:
A Celebration of Life's Most Enduring Relationship

Liberated Parents/Liberated Children:
Your Guide to a Happier Family

How to Talk So Kids Will Listen & Listen So Kids Will Talk

Siblings Without Rivalry: How to Help Your Children
Live Together So You Can Live Too

How to Talk So Kids Can Learn: At Home and at School

How to Be the Parent You Always Wanted to Be

How to Talk So Teens Will Listen
& Listen So Teens Will Talk

Books for Children

Bobby and the Brockles

Bobby and the Brockles Go to School

Visit Adele Faber and Elaine Mazlish at
www.fabermazlish.com

How to Be the Parent You Always Wanted to Be

Adele Faber &
Elaine Mazlish

Illustrations by
Kimberly Ann Coe

SCRIBNER
New York • London • Toronto • Sydney • New Delhi

Scribner
A Division of Simon & Schuster, Inc.
1230 Avenue of the Americas
New York, NY 10020

This is a revised and updated version of a work previously published
in 1992 by Hyperion.

First Scribner trade paperback edition October 2013

Manufactured in the United States of America

10 9 8 7 6 5 4 3 2 1

Library of Congress Control Number: 2013023391

ISBN 978-1-4516-6390-7
ISBN 978-1-4516-6392-1 (ebook)

Illustration on page 47 courtesy of Sam Faber Manning.
Illustration on page 60 courtesy of Coco Faber.
Illustration on page 87 courtesy of Andrew Manning.

Contents

Dear Friend,

This was a book that dawned upon us slowly.

The first inkling we had of the need for it came years after our earlier books had won awards and climbed to the top of best-seller lists. We were in a packed auditorium. The night before we had described and dramatized the communication skills that formed the heart of a caring, mutually respectful relationship between parent and child. Now, the morning after, in every part of the auditorium, hands were up and waving. People couldn't wait to tell what they had tried and how thrilled they were with the results. "It was amazing!" . . . "I couldn't believe my ears!" . . . "This stuff really works!"

In the midst of the glow of all the sweet tales of success, one woman frowned.

"Okay, this is great, but what do I do about my husband?"

"Tell him what you learned here last night."

"He'd never listen to me."

"How about giving him one of our books?"

"He'd never read a book."

"Even if it was short?"

"Maybe. But it would have to be really short."

A man raised his hand. "I heard you two speak last year, and I stayed on the next day for the workshop. I have to admit, I was a fantastic parent after that . . . for about a week."

"And then?"

"I reverted. That's why I'm here today. I'm hoping this time it will stick."

Someone changed the subject, and we launched into the

topic of our morning workshop. But those two reactions kept nagging at us and triggered a long discussion on the plane ride home:

How exactly do we help parents in these time-starved times learn new ways to talk to their kids?

How do we give them a sense of what a profound difference some simple skills can make in all their relationships?

How do we help them hang on to what they've learned in a popular culture that's saturated with put-downs, preaching, threats, name-calling, and sarcasm?

The book and CD you are now holding in your hand is the result of that discussion. It is an introduction to our work that will give you a chance to experiment, practice, and make these empowering new methods a natural part of you. It can also serve as a refresher for those of you who want to review and sharpen your skills. As an added bonus, it can be shared with the important people in your child's life—grandparents, relatives, nanny, babysitter, and of course, your spouse.

It isn't easy to change deeply ingrained ways of talking, especially when we're tired, stressed, frustrated, or just plain exhausted. It is our hope that this combination of CD, cartoons, stories, and simple exercises will give you some of the know-how you need to cope with one of the most challenging and important jobs in the world.

Warmest wishes,
Adele Faber
Elaine Mazlish

Part I

Principles and Skills

About Feelings

"What bothers me about kids is how they cry and carry on over the least little thing. And there's no reasoning with them."

About Feelings

When their unhappy feelings are denied or dismissed, children often become more upset.

Even a logical solution from the parent doesn't seem to help.

Children Want You to Know What They're Feeling

Sometimes it helps if you just listen.

Sometimes a word, like "oh" or "mmm," lets them know you understand.

Sometimes it helps if you can name the feeling.

Most children appreciate it when you give them in fantasy what they can't have in reality.

You can accept children's feelings even when you need to stop or limit their actions.

Practice Acknowledging Feelings

Part I

In each of the following examples, choose the response that shows you understand.

1. CHILD: Daddy nearly killed me when he took that splinter out of my finger.

PARENT: a) It couldn't have been that bad.
b) Sounds as if it really hurt.
c) He did it for your own good.

2. CHILD: Just because of a little snow, the coach canceled our big game.

PARENT: a) That must be a disappointment. You were all psyched to play and now you have to wait.
b) Don't let it get you down. You'll have plenty of other chances to play.
c) Your coach made the right decision. Sometimes a little snow can turn into a big snow.

3. A child is playing with your new string of beads.

PARENT: a) How many times have I told you never to touch my jewelry? You're a bad girl.
b) Please don't play with Mommy's beads. You'll break them.
c) You really like my new beads. The problem is, they break easily. You can play with these wooden beads or with this scarf.

4. **CHILD:** I don't like spiders.
PARENT: a) Oh.
b) Why not? They're part of nature.
c) I don't like them either.

5. **CHILD:** (*looking anxious*) I have to take my math final tomorrow.
PARENT: a) Relax. I'm sure you'll do well.
b) If you had spent more time studying, you wouldn't be worried now.
c) You sound worried. I'll bet you wish it were over and done with.

6. Your child is eating spaghetti with his/her fingers.
PARENT: a) Your table manners are disgusting.
b) I know it's tempting to eat with your fingers. When the family eats together, I'd like you to use a fork.
c) I can't believe that at your age you're still eating with your fingers.

7. **CHILD:** David wants to take me to the school dance. He's really nice, but I don't know . . .
PARENT: a) Oh go. You'll see, you'll have fun.
b) Well make up your mind. Either you want to go or you don't.
c) So, part of you wants to go and part of you isn't sure.

8. CHILD: I'm gonna run away from home.
PARENT: a) Fine, I'll help you pack.
b) You're being silly. I don't want to hear that kind of talk.
c) You sound very unhappy. I'll bet you wish a lot of things were different around here.

Answers: 1b, 2a, 3c, 4a, 5c, 6b, 7c, 8c

Practice Acknowledging Feelings

Part II

Under each of the following statements, write

a) an unhelpful response
b) a helpful response that acknowledges feelings

1. "I'm never going to play with Susie again!"

Unhelpful: ______________________________
____
____
____

Helpful: ______________________________
____
____
____

2 ."How come my sister gets so many birthday presents?"

Unhelpful: ______________________________
____
____
____

Helpful: ______________________________
____
____
____

3. "This picture I made is ugly."

Unhelpful: ____

____

____

____

Helpful: ____

____

____

____

4. "My teacher gives us too many tests."

Unhelpful: ____

____

____

____

Helpful: ____

____

____

____

5. A child looks unhappy.

Unhelpful: ____

____

____

____

Helpful: ____

____

____

____

Possible Answers

Here are some responses to the child's statements on the previous pages. There is no such thing as one "correct" answer. As long as we acknowledge a child's feelings with respect, we are helpful.

1. "I'm never going to play with Susie again!"

Unhelpful: You don't really mean that. Susie is your best friend.

Helpful: Something she did made you angry!

2. "How come my sister gets so many birthday presents?"

Unhelpful: Well, on your birthday you'll get presents and your sister won't.

Helpful: It can be hard to watch your sister get all those presents. It could make you wish today were your birthday.

3. "This picture I made is ugly."

Unhelpful: No it isn't. It's beautiful.

Helpful: I can see you're not at all satisfied with the way your picture turned out.

4. "My teacher gives too many tests."

Unhelpful: You complain about everything.
Helpful: If it were up to you, there would be far fewer tests.

5. A child looks unhappy.

Unhelpful: What's wrong? If you don't tell me what's wrong, I can't help you.
Helpful: Something is wrong. Something is making you sad.

About Engaging **Cooperation**

"I get so frustrated when
I tell the kids to do something
and they completely ignore me!"

About Engaging Cooperation

Children find it hard to cooperate when parents blame, call names, threaten, or give orders.

Some Helpful Ways to Engage a Child's Cooperation

Describe what you see.

Say it with a word.

Give information.

Describe what you feel.

Offer a choice.

Write a note.

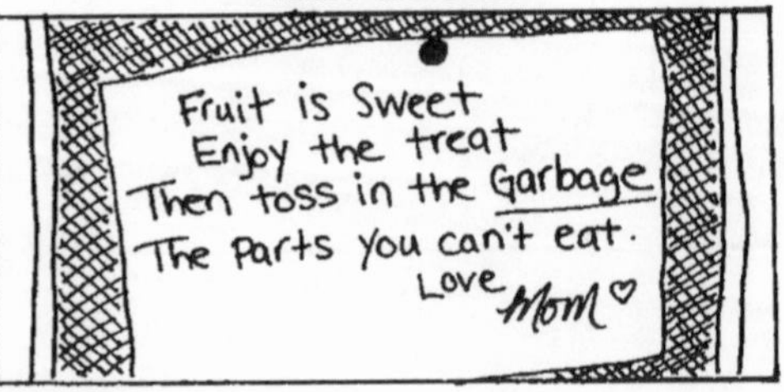

Practice Engaging Cooperation

Part I

In each of the following situations, choose the response most likely to invite cooperation and maintain the child's self-esteem.

1. A child is painting in the living room.

PARENT: a) If I catch you with those paints in the living room once more, I'll take them away.
b) Paint can stain the carpet. You can paint in the kitchen or in your room. You decide.
c) What is wrong with you? Do you know how hard it is to get paint out of a rug?

2. CHILD: (*whining*) Mom, you've got to take me for school supplies today! You said you would.

PARENT: a) Stop that whining!
b) Don't bother me now. Maybe later.
c) Here's how I like to be asked: Mom, could you please take me for school supplies today?

3. A child runs out the door leaving his homework on the table.

PARENT: a) Jimmy, homework!
b) Jimmy, come back here. You are such a scatterbrain! Look what you left on the table.
c) You spent the whole night doing your homework and then you go off without it. That's brilliant!

4. **CHILD:** Mommy, get off the phone. I want to tell you something.

PARENT: a) Leave me alone! Can't I have one conversation in peace?

b) Shhh, be quiet! I'll be off soon.

c) I'd like to finish talking. You can write what you want to tell me or you can draw it.

5. Your child has neglected to water the plant you bought for her.

PARENT: a) You begged me for that plant and now you're letting it die.

b) The leaves on your new plant are drooping.

c) The next plant I buy you is going to be plastic.

Answers: 1b, 2c, 3a, 4c, 5b

Practice Engaging Cooperation

Part II

Your child brushes her teeth and leaves the water dripping in the bathroom sink.

1. What might you say that would not be helpful to his or her self-esteem or to the relationship between you?

____

____

____

2. Show how you might use each of the methods listed below to engage your child's cooperation.

   a) **Describe what you see.**

   ____

   ____

   ____

   b) **Give information.**

   ____

   ____

   ____

c) **Offer a choice.**

____

____

____

d) **Say it with a word.**

____

____

____

e) **Describe what you feel.**

____

____

____

f) **Write a note.**

____

____

____

Possible Answers

Here are some unhelpful responses to the child who has left the water dripping in the bathroom sink:

Who left the water running?

How many times do I have to remind you to shut the faucet?

Why are you so careless?

It's because of people like you that we have a water shortage.

Here are some responses that might invite cooperation and leave both parent and child feeling good about themselves and each other:

a) **Describe what you see.**

The water is dripping.

b) **Give information.**

Even a slow drip can waste gallons of water each day.

c) **Offer a choice.**

You can shut the faucet with your right hand or your left hand.

d) **Say it with a word.**
The faucet.

e) **Describe what you feel.**
It bothers me to see precious water being wasted.

f) **Write a note.**

If you hear a drip, drip, drip,
To the sink *quick* make a trip,
Don't let the water get away,
Save it for another day.

Thank you,
The Management

(Kids love rhymes, but a simple "Please shut faucet after use" or HELP END DRIPS can also be effective.)

An Alternative to Punishment

"When a child does something really bad, shouldn't he be punished? How else will he learn?"

The Problem with Punishment

Many parents believe that the way to discipline a child who has misbehaved is to punish him. These parents are convinced that that's the only way a child will "learn a lesson."

But most children don't react that way to being punished.

Some children think . . .

Other children think . . .

Others think . . .

Problem Solving

How can parents motivate their children to behave responsibly? Are there alternatives to punishment? One alternative is to sit down with a child and work at solving the problem together. Here's how the problem-solving method works:

Step I. Listen to and acknowledge your child's feelings and needs.

Don't criticize what he says. Encourage him to explore all his feelings.

Sum up your child's point of view.

Step II. Talk about your feelings or needs. (It's best to keep this part brief.)

Step III. Invite your child to join you in a search for solutions.

Step IV. Write down all ideas. Don't comment on whether they're good or bad. (If possible, let the child go first.)

Step V. Decide which ideas you don't like, which you do, and how you plan to follow through.

Practice with Problem Solving

Imagine that you have a six-year-old daughter, Amy, who is too rough with your eighteen-month-old son, Billy. You've warned Amy over and over again not to hurt her brother, but she just ignores you. It's true, sometimes Billy grabs her toys, but you've explained to Amy that her brother is only a baby and doesn't understand. Today Billy tore a page of her favorite book and Amy pushed him so hard that he fell and got a bump on the back of his head. There seems nothing left to do but punish her. But how? You could hit her the way she hits her brother. Or you could forbid her to play with her friends for a week. Or you could take away her new toy.

Instead, you decide to listen respectfully to her point of view, share your point of view, and ask her to join you in trying to solve the problem together.

Step I. Listen to and acknowledge your child's feelings and needs. *For example, here's what you might say to bring up the subject:*

PARENT: I notice that when Billy grabs your toys, it makes you so mad that you either hit him or push him. Have I got that right?

And here's how your child might respond:

CHILD: Right! He is such a pest. He bothers me all the time. He tore my best book. I *had* to push him. He should play with his own baby toys.

PARENT: **(Continue the conversation by acknowledging your child's feelings.)**

____

____

____

____

PARENT: **(Find out if there's anything else her brother does that bothers her.)**

____

____

____

____

CHILD: **(What might she add?)**

____

____

____

____

PARENT: **(Sum up your child's point of view.)**

____

____

____

____

Step II. Talk about your feelings or needs. Keep it brief.

PARENT: ______________________________

Step III. Invite your child to join you in a search for solutions.

PARENT: ______________________________

Step IV. Write down all ideas. Don't comment on whether they're good or bad. If possible, let the child go first. *For example:*

send him to live with Grandma

Step V. Decide which ideas you don't like, which you do, and how you plan to follow through.

PARENT: ______________________________

CHILD: ______________________________

PARENT: ______________________________

CHILD: ______________________________

Step VI. Shake hands on your agreement.

Solving the Problem Together

Here's our version of the kind of problem-solving discussion that might take place between a parent and a child who is hitting a younger sibling.

Step I. Listen to and acknowledge your child's feelings and needs.

PARENT: I notice that when Billy grabs your toys, it makes you so mad that you either hit him or push him. Have I got that right?

CHILD: Right! He is such a pest. He tore my best book. I *had* to push him. He should play with his own baby toys.

PARENT: (*acknowledging the child's feelings*) So when you hit him, it's your way of saying, "Don't break or tear my things. Play with your own toys and leave me alone."

CHILD: Yeah.

PARENT: (*finding out if there's anything else the child wants to add*) Is there anything else Billy does that bothers you? I'd really like to know.

CHILD: The time I let him play with my puzzle, he lost two pieces. And he threw my teddy bear in the toilet.

PARENT: (*summing up child's point of view*) So not only does he bother you when you're playing, but when you try to be nice to him, he either loses your toys or ruins them.

Step II. Talk about your feelings.

PARENT: Here's how it is from my point of view. I get very upset when one of my children hurts another of my children.

Step III. Invite your child to join you in a search for solutions.

PARENT: Let's put our heads together and see if we can think of some ways for you to play peacefully, to keep your toys safe, and at the same time, make sure your brother doesn't get hurt.

Step IV. Write down *all* ideas. Don't comment on whether they're good or bad. (If possible, let the child go first.)

CHILD: Send him to live with Grandma.

PARENT: I'll write that down. What else?

CHILD: Make him stay in his crib.

PARENT: (*writing*) Stay in his crib. Okay, anything else?

CHILD: I could close my door.

PARENT: (*writing*) Close door. We could put the toys you don't want him to touch on a high shelf that he can't reach.

CHILD: Or put them in my closet.

PARENT: I've got that. But what can you do when he takes a book that's special to you?

CHILD: I could tell him, "That's *my* book!" and give him another one that I don't mind him touching.

PARENT: (*still writing*) And if you want to play by yourself, you can tell him, "I want to play by myself now."

Step V. Decide which ideas you don't like, which you do like, and how you plan to follow through.

PARENT: Well, I couldn't go along with this first idea of sending him to Grandma. I could never send either of my children away. So we'd better cross that out.

CHILD: And if we make him stay in his crib, he'll just cry. So cross that out too.

PARENT: But you could close your door if you want to be private.

CHILD: And we could hide my best toys in the closet.

PARENT: Do you think you could restrain him gently if he tries to grab a toy you don't want him to touch?

CHILD: Yeah, but what if I give him another toy or tell him I want to play by myself and he still won't listen?

PARENT: If you try everything we've talked about and it still doesn't work, you can always call me and I'll take him out of your room. But I have the feeling you'll get better and better at figuring out ways to handle Billy gently by yourself.

Step VI. Parent and child shake hands on their agreement.

PARENT: Let's shake on the ideas we agreed to and put them up on the refrigerator door to help us both remember.

What If the Solution Doesn't Work?

Sometimes parents ask, "What if the plan you and your child agree upon works for a while and then fails? Suppose the child reverts to her old ways? What then?"

These are the times that test our determination. We can either go back to lecturing and punishing or we can go back to the drawing board. For example:

PARENT: I'm disappointed that our ideas aren't working anymore. I see you've started to hit Billy again and that's not acceptable. Shall we give the old plan another chance? Shall we talk about what's getting in the way? Or do we need to come up with some new ideas?

As parents, we realize that even the most perfect plan will not be permanent. What worked for the child when she was six may not work for her when she turns seven. Life is a continual process of adjustment and readjustment—of having to cope with new problems. By involving our children in the search for solutions, we are giving them the tools to help them solve the problems that confront them now—while they're at home—and in the difficult, complex world that awaits them.

About **Praise**

"Sometimes my kids like it when I praise them. And sometimes they don't. Is there something I'm missing?"

Some Kinds of Praise
Can Make Kids Feel Worse

Why do my kids brush me off when I praise them? I tell my daughter she's smart and she says, "Lisa is smarter." I tell her she's beautiful and she says, "I'm fat." I tell her she's a fantastic big sister, a gifted artist, and she punches her sister and tells me she can't draw. It's like she's out to prove me wrong.

It's worse with my son. He was shooting baskets and finally managed to sink one. I yelled, "Perfect! You're a natural!" He put the ball down and went into the house. I don't get it. Every time I try to praise my kids, it seems to have the opposite effect.

You just put your finger on the problem with the kind of global praise that evaluates kids. Words like "smart," "beautiful," and "perfect" not only make them focus on everything that's wrong with them, it can even discourage them from continuing to try. After all, if I'm perfect now, why risk the possibility of messing up next time?

Does that mean I should quit praising them?

It means if we want to encourage our kids to believe in themselves, to continue to persist, we need to steer clear of words that evaluate, like "good," "great," "fantastic," "the best!" Instead, we can tell ourselves to simply describe. *You can describe what you see or describe what you feel.*

Describe What You See

- "You stuck with that problem until you solved it!"
- "Hey, you nailed that shot! It sailed right into the basket!"
- "Even though you had your own work to do, you helped your sister with her homework."

Describe What You Feel

- "I love your 'sunset at sea' painting. It gives me a happy, peaceful feeling."

- "I have to laugh every time I think about that joke you told me."

The result of describing what we see or what we feel is almost magical. It not only affirms our children's efforts, it helps them to believe in themselves. Best of all, it gives them the courage and motivation to continue their efforts. Their inner message becomes loud and clear: "I don't give up until I solve a problem." . . . "The more I practice, the better I get!" . . . "I can be kind, even when I'm under pressure." . . . "I can tell a funny joke" . . . "paint a beautiful sunset."

No doubt about it. Descriptive praise can be potent stuff for building confident, caring kids.

Here's another variation for your praise toolbox:

Sum Up What You See in a Word

- "You didn't stop working on that piece until you learned every note. That's what I call *persistence.*"
- "I see you left that last piece of cake for your sister. Now that's *willpower*!"
- "You raked all the leaves and bagged them. And without being asked! That's what I call *taking responsibility*."

But suppose there's nothing to praise? Suppose the school bus is on its way, and she still isn't dressed . . . or he complains that his teacher gives too much homework and there's no way he could ever finish it all.

These are the moments when we're sorely tempted to tell the children what's wrong with them:

- "Why does it take you forever to get dressed? Look at you! You're still barefoot! At this rate you'll never make the bus!"
- "If you had started your homework when I told you to,

instead of playing that stupid video game, you'd be done by now. But no, you look for any excuse to procrastinate!"

Instead, we can reverse course and tell ourselves to describe to the children what they *have* accomplished, however much or however little.

- "You dressed yourself, finished your breakfast, and brushed your teeth. All you have left to do is to find your shoes and socks, and you're ready to go!"
- "Let's see . . . ten problems involving addition and subtraction of fractions. That can be wearying. But I see you already figured out the answers to the first two. It looks like you're on your way."

By pointing out whatever progress they have made, large or small, we give our children the courage to continue to persevere.

But suppose there really is absolutely nothing to praise. And suppose you have one of these super-sensitive kids who goes to pieces when he does anything wrong.

Help him realize that his mistake could be an important discovery. One mother told how her three-year-old son was happily shaking his sippy cup as he was talking to her. Suddenly the lid flew off, and juice squirted all over him and the floor. The little boy began to sob hysterically.

"Sammy," his mother exclaimed dramatically, *"you found out!"*

He stopped crying and stared at her in confusion.

Very slowly, she said, "You found out that when you shake a sippy cup, the lid can fall off and the juice will come flying out everywhere!"

The following week, when Grandma came to visit, she put

her pocketbook, packages, and sunglasses on the kitchen counter. Moments later, she reached for one of her packages and her glasses fell to the floor. As she exclaimed, "Oh no!" and bent to pick them up, Sammy tugged at her jacket. With great excitement he told her, "Grandma, you found out!"

"Found out?" she questioned.

"You found out," he explained, "when you leave your glasses on the edge of the counter, they can fall off!"

"Hmm," Grandma said admiringly. "I'll have to remember that!"

Practice Descriptive Praise

Part I

Choose the statement you think would be most likely to help a child believe in himself.

1. a) You were the best one in the whole play.
   b) From the moment you stepped on the stage, the whole audience was laughing and focused on your every word.

2. a) I like the way the colors in your shirt and pants go together.
   b) You always dress so beautifully.

3. a) Your penmanship isn't all bad. It just needs work. Your words are scrunched together and your letters are all over the place.
   b) These letters here are sitting right on the line. And these three words are especially easy to read because there are big spaces between them.

4. a) You saw how busy I was and cleared the table without being asked. I really appreciate that.
   b) You're always so helpful.

5. a) If you had read the label before you washed your sweater, it would still fit you.
   b) You found out that hot water really does shrink a wool sweater.

6. a) Thanks for calling to let me know you'll be late. That saved me a lot of worry.
   b) I can always count on you to be thoughtful.

7. a) A hundred on your math test! You are so smart!
   b) You stuck with those problems until you figured out the answer to every one of them. That's what I call perseverance!

8. a) When it was time for the nurse to draw your blood, you didn't even flinch! You held out your arm and made it easy for her to find the vein.
   b) I'm proud of you. You're a brave boy!

9. a) Thanks for shoveling all that heavy snow. It made it a lot easier for me to get the car out of the driveway.
   b) Good job!

10. a) You're always so generous.
    b) What a nice surprise! You made enough popcorn for everyone.

Answers: 1b, 2a, 3b, 4a, 5b, 6a, 7b, 8a, 9a, 10b

Practice Descriptive Praise

Part II

For each situation, write an appreciative descriptive comment that could help a child recognize his strengths:

1. It is your son's birthday. He eagerly opens the present his friend gives him. It is a video game he already owns. He thanks his friend for the present.

   Your comment:

   ____

   ____

   ____

2. Your daughter sits down to practice her new piano piece soon after she comes home from school.

   Your comment:

   ____

   ____

   ____

3. Your son loves pasta. When the serving bowl is passed around, he starts to empty it all onto his plate. Suddenly he stops, looks around, and puts some back in the bowl.

   Your comment:

   ____

   ____

   ____

4. Your toddler pats the dog very gently.

   Your comment:

   ____

   ____

   ____

5. Your teenager leaves a note on the kitchen table, telling you where he's gone and when he'll be back.

   Your comment:

   ____

   ____

   ____

6. Your preschooler uses his napkin to wipe his mouth instead of his sleeve.

   Your comment:

   ____

   ____

   ____

Possible Answers

1. "You didn't tell your friend that you already have that video game. That was kind of you to care about his feelings."
2. "You sat down to practice your new piano piece without a single reminder from anyone. That's what I call self-discipline!"
3. "Even though you love pasta, when you noticed there might not be enough for everyone, you put some of yours back. That was really considerate."
4. "You patted Barney so very gently today. His wagging tail tells you how much he liked it."
5. "That note you left saved me a lot of worry. Thanks for taking the time to be super clear and specific."
6. "You didn't use your sleeve to wipe your mouth even once! You remembered to reach for your napkin every time."

About **Anger**

"Every morning I vow that
today will be different.
Today I'll be a kind, patient,
loving parent. And every
morning I turn into a
horrible, screaming maniac."

YOU ARE DRIVING ME CRAZY!

About Anger

How do I handle my anger? No matter how hard I try to control myself, I end up saying or doing things I deeply regret.

Parenting is high-stress work. Kids can be infuriating. Telling ourselves not to feel what we feel can only add to our rage and despair. The challenge is to figure out how to express our savage feelings in ways that offer us some relief and do no damage to the children.

Here are some experiences and discoveries that were helpful to us:

Run for Your Life!

A mother in our parent guidance group, led by child psychologist Dr. Haim Ginott, was the first to speak. She was clearly agitated.

"Dr. Ginott, I was so angry at my son this morning, I didn't know whether to hit him or kill him!"

"If there's ever a choice between hitting and killing," said Dr. Ginott, "hit!"

We all laughed. "But basically, I'm opposed to hitting," he continued. "What does a child learn when his father turns him over his knee and emphasizes each word with each blow: 'This will teach you, once and for all, *never* to hit anyone smaller than yourself!'"

"I know . . . I know . . . you've told us a hundred times. 'Children learn what they live.' But what else could I do? What would *you* do?"

Dr. Ginott drew himself up to his full height, raised his hand in a threatening gesture, and spoke fiercely to an imaginary child. "I am so angry . . . sooo angry, I am about to hit! . . . So *quick, run for your life*!"

We laughed again, but the following week the same mother began the session by reporting a triumph to the group. "I did it!" she exclaimed. "I was so furious with my son, Tony, for waking the baby and making her cry, I yelled your exact words at him. And he ran!

"Two minutes later he poked his head in the room and asked, 'Can I come back now?' 'Not yet!' I said sternly. 'Not until you figure out a way to help your sister feel better again!' The next time I looked up, he was walking around with a blanket on his head, making silly noises, and playing peek-a-boo with the baby. She laughed every time he whipped the blanket off his head."

After congratulating the mother, there was general agreement that we couldn't rely on any one tactic, that instead of telling ourselves not to feel what we felt, we needed to be able to vent our intense feelings by putting the skills we had already learned into action.

Everyone had a favorite method.

Say It in a Word.

I used to get more and more frustrated as I reminded my teenager, for the tenth time, to hang up his jacket instead of dropping it on the floor . . . to turn off the light when he leaves the bathroom . . . to lower the volume on the music he's blasting, etc. Now, instead of going into my usual long lecture, I just yell what's upsetting me with a single word:

"Jeff, the **jacket!**"
"Jeff, the **light!**"
"The **music!**" . . . "The **volume!**" . . ."**MY EARS!**"

It works. Yelling that one word gives me some relief and gets his attention. Best of all, instead of tuning me out, it gives him a chance to tell himself what to do.

Say What You Don't Like.
Add What You Would Like or Expect.

- "*I don't like* seeing the cat's tail pulled! *I expect* kindness to animals! And you can start right now!"
- "*I don't like* seeing all of the mashed potatoes disappear onto one person's plate. *I expect* everyone to make sure that each of us gets a fair share!"
- "*I don't like* having to hunt for my scissors. *I expect* the person who borrowed them to return them to the same place he found them!"

Use Big Words.

Consider Dr. Ginott's suggestion to use your anger to increase your children's vocabulary. You'll gain some emotional relief and your children will do better on their college entrance tests. The English language is rich in words that describe a range of our feelings, from mild irritation to full-blown rage: "I am irked . . . vexed . . . irritated . . . aggravated . . . exasperated . . . appalled . . . incensed . . . dismayed . . . livid . . . infuriated . . . full of consternation!"

Dr. Ginott reported that he once said to a misbehaving boy in his play therapy session, "I am feeling *acrimonious*!"

"Whatever it is," the boy responded, "I better get out of here!"

Forget About Being Calm.
Describe the Problem and Feel Free to Roar.

- "Three people are still waiting to get into the bathroom!"
- "It's freezing in here! Someone left the door wide open!"
- "I just mopped the kitchen floor and now it's covered with muddy footprints!"

State the Rule. Follow Up with a Choice. If Necessary, Take Action.

Billy, age six, is sitting at the dinner table, playing with his food.

FATHER: Billy, food is for eating, not for playing with.

Billy takes a mouthful of food, spits it out, and laughs.

FATHER: **No spitting food at the dinner table! It upsets your mother and makes me angry!**

Billy is startled, but after a moment he grins and sticks out the tip of his tongue as if to spit again.

FATHER: Billy, here are your choices:

1. If you're in no mood for acceptable behavior, you can leave the table and play in your room.
2. If you're still hungry, you can stay and eat without spitting. Let me know what you decide.

BILLY: Stay.

Seconds later Billy laughs, takes a bite of bread, and spits it in his father's face.

FATHER: (*as he grabs his son firmly and deposits him in his room*) This is funny to you, but not to me. I can see you're not so hungry tonight.

Beware the Word "You."

When we're angry, stress hormones flood our bodies. We experience a powerful urge to attack! The first word that springs to our lips is "you."

What is wrong with *you*!
Now look what *you* did!
You did it again!
You never . . .
You always . . .

The accusing "you" cuts like a knife. Instead of thinking about what's wrong and how to make it right, the child focuses on self-defense and counterattack: "No, I don't" . . . "It wasn't me" . . . "It's because of you" . . . "You blame me for everything" . . . "You're mean" . . . "I hate you!"

When Possible, Substitute an "I" for a "You."

We have a better chance of discharging our strong feelings and getting through to our kids if we reach for an "I" and state what we feel or need. Put yourself in a child's shoes. Check the statement you'd be more likely to consider.

a) "You are a pest!"
b) "I need to rest."

a) "You're bad!"
b) "I'm mad!"

a) "You are so rude! You always interrupt."
b) "I get so frustrated when I'm interrupted! I lose my train of thought."

a) "You are an inconsiderate slob!"
b) "When I get home after a long day at work and see sneakers on the table, a sink full of dirty dishes, and crumbs all over the floor, I get so discouraged, I don't even feel like starting dinner!"

Chances are, you checked "b" in every case. As long as we're not being personally attacked, it's usually easier to respond helpfully to what someone else feels or needs.

"You Can Be a Little Nicer Than You Feel, but Not Much."

Those words from Dr. Ginott took a long time to sink in. Most of us are determined to be loving and patient parents. When negative feelings arise, we push them away and soldier on. Big mistake.

I (Adele) still remember the time I was sitting outside on a hot summer afternoon, reading a magazine, finally resting and enjoying a moment of peace after cleaning the house. Suddenly my five-year-old ran over, flung himself onto my lap, and enthusiastically announced, "I love you, Mommy!"

How very sweet! And how very annoying! "And your mommy loves you," I made myself say as he shifted position, knocked over my magazine, and tugged at my hair. This went on for a few minutes when suddenly I heard myself yelling, *"Get off!"* and flinging him to the ground.

One look at his bewildered face and I was sick with guilt. What was wrong with me? What kind of monster mother was I? Then I remembered. *"You can be a little nicer than you feel, but not much."* I needed to protect both myself and my son from my strong feelings.

Moments later it happened again. This time I was prepared. As soon as he plopped down on my lap and declared his love, I said, "I am such a lucky mom," and firmly removed him.

"But Mommy," he protested, "I love you!"

"I'm really happy to hear that. Right now I need to sit by myself and read."

"But Mommy!"

"Here's an idea. You can show me your feelings with a drawing . . . or a song."

"No, I don't want to draw," he said, and went off to play with his sister.

Everyone in the group laughed in recognition and everyone had a story to tell of sitting on their real feelings and exploding moments later. The ongoing challenge for all was to tune into the scary power of our angry feelings so we could protect our children from them.

Here's another mom's account of what happened when she tried to apply her new knowledge:

Show Me How to Have a Tantrum.

I grew up in an abusive family. That's why I was so determined never to do to my kids what was done to me. Anyway, I woke up one morning in a really bad mood. I called the kids in, told them I was in a mean-mad mood, that it had nothing to do with them, that I just felt like yelling at everyone and blaming everyone for everything, that none of it was their fault, but it was a good idea to stay away from me so they didn't get hurt.

They both looked at me with big eyes and disappeared into their rooms. That helped a little, but still, I was boiling inside. About a minute later, Josh, my five-year-old, came out to get something. I stopped him and asked, "Josh, you know how to have a tantrum?"

"Sure," he said.

I said, "Show me how to have a tantrum."

He threw himself on the floor and kicked and screamed. I threw myself down next to him and screamed right along with him. Megan, my seven-year-old, came into the room and asked, "What's going on?"

Josh stopped for a moment and announced, "I'm showing Mom how to have a tantrum."

Megan said, "Oh," and lay down next to us, and we all yelled and thrashed around together. You can probably

> guess how it all ended up. You're right. By the time it was over, we were all laughing and feeling a whole lot better.

And Still We Explode?

Yes. It can happen. Even to the most loving and determined of us. No matter how much planning we do, how deeply we care, or how skillful we are, life's pressures and tensions can suddenly boil up and over, leading us to say or do things that might normally horrify us.

So what are our options? Shall we beat up on ourselves for our failures, or should we say, "Guilt, go away! Buzz off! I get the message. Now I have to think about why I exploded. Is there something I can do to prevent it from happening again? Is there a way to make amends for what did happen? How do I get back to the relationship I want to have?"

A Grandmother's Experience

Sometimes a simple conversation is all that's needed. Here's what one grandmother told us:

> My six-year-old grandson is autistic. I love to visit and play with him, but the last time I was there, he suddenly climbed up on the back of the couch and began jumping up and down on the edge. Right behind him was a half-open window. I was so frightened that I screamed at him to get off. He kept right on jumping so I grabbed him and pulled him off and held him down until his mother came in.
>
> Since then he's refused to talk to me. When he sees me, he runs away.
>
> Last week I decided to try again. I said (to his back since he wouldn't look at me), "I've been thinking about what happened last time, and I feel bad about it. I want us to be friends again."

He turned around and said, "Me too."

And that was it. It was over, and we were back to our old relationship.

A Mom's Explosion and the Road Back

This next example comes from an e-mail exchange with a troubled mom who coincidentally had been leading a How to Talk So Kids Will Listen workshop group. Here are some excerpts from our correspondence:

> My friend and I decided to give our kids a special treat this summer. We loaded up the car, got everyone buckled in, and headed off to a local farm to do some peach picking. About ten minutes into the trip, my oldest (he's seven) started tormenting the younger kids in the backseat. One of them began crying. Another was screaming.
>
> What do I do? I say his name a few times. He ignores me. I let him know that screaming in the car makes it dangerous to drive. Again, I'm ignored. I tell the kids he's picking on, "If you don't like what he's doing, you can tell him to stop." They tell him and he ignores them too. Everyone is getting more and more upset.
>
> My insides are boiling. I am thinking, what do I do now? We're driving on the highway; I can't stop. He's making everyone miserable; he won't stop. Should I pull over? Is it safe? I am truly at a loss.
>
> Finally we get to the farm. I pull him aside and express my outrage in words that I'm too embarrassed to repeat in an e-mail. Somehow I manage to let him know that I expect the rest of the afternoon to be completely different! Things did get better, but I told myself I must have some kind of follow-up. Do you have any thoughts or guidance for me? I would appreciate anything you have to offer.

My Response.

Ah, it's experiences like these that keep us from getting smug. Sometimes we find ourselves stuck in a miserable situation where there are simply no good answers. But the beauty of this approach is that we can usually figure out how to prevent it from happening again. Here's one possibility that might be helpful:

Find the right moment to approach your son. Say, "I need to talk to you about the last time we all went peach picking. You know what happened and you know how upset and frightened I was. I felt as if everybody's life in that car was in danger and I had no way to stop it. I never want to go through that again, so here are the choices I can think of:

1. I leave you at home with a babysitter.
2. You give me, in writing, a list of ideas that you're willing to put into action for keeping everybody peaceful and happy on our next car trip. Think about it and let me know what you decide.

It may be that your big boy isn't even ready to consider the options you offer, that he first needs to vent some of the hostile feelings he might be having about his siblings, and that what's really needed between the two of you is a problem-solving session. You'll know only by wading into the issue.

I'd be interested in knowing what route you finally decide to take.

Her Answer

I walked around for days smiling, just thinking about the brilliance of your advice. Thank you!

It took a while to find the right time to talk, but I opened the conversation with your words exactly. It turns out your hunch was right on the mark. The first words out of his mouth were about how his spot in the car (between a car seat and a booster) was much too tight for him, and how he was so uncomfortable that he had to keep pushing and shoving the other kids away. Considering this new information, we came up with ideas about what to do when we don't feel comfortable and how to be peaceful during a long car ride.

So far so good. But more important than any specific results, my son felt understood. Now he knows his mother is willing to give him the time to work things out. What a great feeling for both of us!

When I met with the parents in my *How to Talk* workshop group, I described my problem to them and quoted the first part of your e-mail response to me: "Sometimes we find ourselves stuck in a miserable situation where there are simply no good answers. But the beauty of this approach is that we can usually figure out how to prevent it from happening again."

If only I could share how far-reaching and comforting those words have been both to me and to all the parents in my groups. Even if we do explode, there is a way back!

Part II

Questions and Answers

Parents Ask . . .

Whenever we give a program on communication skills to parents, we stop at one point and invite the audience to tell us what's on their minds. After a second of silence, hands fly up everywhere. The sheer number of comments, questions, and urgent concerns remind us how overwhelming the challenges of child rearing can be, and how despite all the ground we've already covered in our talk, there's always more—much more—yet to be explored. On the chance that some of the concerns expressed by our audiences are your concerns as well, we'd like to share with you the questions we're most often asked, along with our answers:

What do I do about my two-year-old? Her favorite word is "no!" Just getting her socks on every morning is an exhausting battle.

There's no winning a power struggle with a two-year-old. Since you can't change her mind, consider changing the mood. Go for "funny stuff." Use another voice or accent. Put your hand in her sock and have your sock puppet shriek, "No, no, do not put those smelly toes in me!" Scold the sock as you pull it on. Insist that it do its job and keep your little girl's feet toasty warm. Have fun continuing the drama with the rest of her clothes.

No doubt about it. Anything that's silly, playful, surprising, or comical has the power to melt resistance and invite cooperation. It's something to keep in mind for children and grownups of all ages.

Why would a three-year-old who has never been spanked or slapped suddenly hit his mother? The first time my son did that was while we were playing. I yelled, "Ow! Why did you do that?" and he cried and did it again.

Kids hit. They hit their parents, their siblings, their peers. When they're young (two or three), they become confused and upset if you scold or protest. Often they cry. ("Why is my mother yelling at me?") Not until they're about seven do they develop the *consistent* ability to put themselves in someone else's shoes and imagine what another person might be feeling. In the meantime, your job is to repeat endless variations of "No hitting!" . . . "I don't like that!" . . . "I will not let you hit me." . . . "Tell me what you want with *words*." Then be sure to suggest the words: "You can tell me, 'Stop! It hurts when *you* brush my hair! I want to do it myself!'"

One dad proudly reported seeing his four-year-old, about to strike his little sister yet again, suddenly shout "*Words!*" To him, it was a sign of monumental progress.

My daughter has been doing a lot of whining lately and it's driving me crazy. How can I stop it?

Before you try to stop the whining, you might want to think about what could be causing it. Is the whining a symptom of tiredness . . . hunger . . . jealousy . . . frustration . . . anger? Once you've zeroed in on the cause, you can deal with the feeling by respectfully acknowledging it: "I can hear how disappointed you are that I'm not buying you new skates today. Let me write it down on your wish list."

Sounds easy, doesn't it? It isn't. The sound of a whining child can be torture to listen to and can drive the most patient of parents to lash out at the youngster with, "Stop it! Why can't you talk like a normal person? You are such a whiner."

But by labeling the child a whiner, we reinforce her whining behavior. Instead we want to encourage our children to get their needs met in more direct and positive ways. For example, if your daughter persists in whining, you can tell her: "Lisa, it's hard for me to listen when you have that sound in your voice. Could you ask me again, using your pleasant voice? That will make it much easier for me to hear you and consider what you want."

My son has a tantrum over the least little thing. For example, when it's time to leave the playground, I usually have to carry him out kicking and screaming. How do I keep him from having these tantrums?

A tantrum is a child's response to powerful emotions that temporarily overwhelm him. When your son was forced to leave an activity he loved, he protested this "injustice" with his whole being, by kicking, screaming, and crying. Here are two ways you can help him to keep his emotions from boiling over:

1. Let him have plenty of advance notice of your intentions. This gives him a chance to adjust to the idea of having to make the transition from playing to leaving. For example, "Jimmy, we'll be leaving in ten minutes." And again, five minutes later: "You're having such a good time going down the slide. Too bad we have to leave for home so soon. Do you want to take one more turn on the slide or two more?"
2. You can also give your son in fantasy what you can't give him in reality: "Jimmy, I can see that if it were up to you, you would take ten more turns on the slide. Maybe even a

hundred. Boy, do you wish we didn't have to go home now!" By expressing his wishes in fantasy, you make it a little easier for your son to deal with reality.

One woman told us that she had recently adopted a four-year-old girl named Emily who had constant tantrums, sometimes lasting more than an hour. It seems that Emily's natural mother had died six months before and since then she had had inconsistent care. The adoptive mother said:

> I've been trying to express what I thought Emily was feeling as she was tantruming, but mostly I tried showing her I understood her feelings before the tantrum. "Oh, Emily, that could be frustrating!" or "You must be so upset!" It was as if she never heard me. But last week a miracle happened. We had the perfect setup for a major explosion. Emily had been invited to play with a little girl she had just met in her nursery school but my sister (she drove her) couldn't find the child's house, gave up, and brought Emily home. I took one look at her face (heavy storm clouds) and said, "Oh, no! You must be so disappointed! You were looking forward to going to Sara's house all day today!"
>
> Emily nodded and said, "I'm very sad. Can we go to the park?"
>
> I was amazed at her response and felt terrible to have to disappoint her again. I thought, "This next refusal will really push her over the edge." I kneeled down, put my arm around her, and said, "Emily, I wish with all my heart that we could go to the park right now. The problem is, we can't. I have to go to the dentist."
>
> Her lower lip started quivering. I thought, "Uh-oh, here it comes." But it never did. She took a deep breath and said, "Can I come with you?"
>
> I said, "Definitely yes! And tomorrow I'm getting directions and taking you to Sara's house myself."

Emily broke into a big smile.

That night I told my husband how relieved and happy I was that Emily didn't have another meltdown. My husband said, "Maybe she's growing up."

"Yeah, and maybe I'm helping her," I thought to myself.

I saw my son break a vase in the living room and he denied doing it. What's the best way to handle lying?

A lie usually represents a wish or a fear. Your son wished he hadn't broken your vase and feared your reaction. It's a good idea to deal with the wish or deal with the fear rather than focus on the lying. Notice the difference between these two scenarios:

MOTHER: Who broke this vase? . . . Did you do it?
CHILD: Not me.
MOTHER: Are you sure? Don't lie to me now.
CHILD: No, I swear I didn't.
MOTHER: You're a little liar. I saw you do it and now you're going to be punished.

Instead of trying to trap the child in a lie, it would be best to confront the youngster with the truth:

MOTHER: I saw you throw the ball and break the vase.
CHILD: No I didn't! I swear.
MOTHER: I'm sure you wish it hadn't happened. Danny, I'm upset. I expect you to be able to say "no" to yourself when you're tempted to play with a ball in the living room. Now how do we get this mess cleaned up?
CHILD: I'll get the broom.

By not labeling a child "liar," by accepting his feelings and sharing our own, we make it safe for him to come to us with the truth.

What do you do about a child who refuses to sit still in a car? How do I make him behave?

Whenever you ask yourself, "How do I *make* this child do something," tell yourself you're heading in the wrong direction. A more helpful question would be, "How do I encourage my child to become an active participant in solving the problem?"

One father told us that he had been enraged by his son's "hyper" behavior in the car, despite repeated warnings to the boy to sit still. By the time they got home, the father was furious! He was ready to punish his son by taking away his allowance, or TV privileges, or both. Instead he decided to involve his son in finding a solution. He said:

> Michael, I didn't like what happened in the car today. When you jumped up and down in the backseat, your head blocked the window and I almost didn't see that big truck coming up behind us. That was dangerous. For this family's safety I need you to think of three things you could do in the car that would help you to sit quietly.

To his father's surprise, Michael said he wanted to think of *ten* things. The father wrote down all of Michael's ideas and then posted his list on the dashboard of the car. Here's the list Michael came up with:

1. Look at cars and trucks
2. Sing songs—softly
3. Play games with Daddy like "ABC game" (find alphabet letters on signs along the road)

4. Think
5. Chew gum or eat grapes
6. Count all the things in the car
7. Rest
8. Color
9. Watch people through the car windows
10. Read books

The father said that Michael was very pleased with himself, but the best part was seeing his son read his list and use his own ideas.

I am a mother come from China. Now my most annoy thing is that my son could not keep his promise. He always promise me he will study after half or one hour play, but whenever it is time, he always finds excuse . . . headache, tired, need sleep . . . to give up learning. I angry with him several times, however he finally said, "What you can do to me? I am not study anymore."

He is thirteen years old. I do not know how to do really. I try to explain my awkward situation with my poor English. I am hope to get your instruction. What to do?

Consider taking the problem-solving route. It is hard to get cooperation from a child without first acknowledging his feelings. If you don't care how he feels, why should he care about how upset you are when he doesn't do his homework?

You can start by saying, "When you come home from a long day at school, the *last* thing you want to do is sit down and do more schoolwork! You'd rather be doing *anything* else—playing outside, listening to music, watching TV, eating, just relaxing and doing nothing. Homework is one big pain in the neck. I wish there was no homework! Maybe it should be abolished! (Let him talk about what he doesn't like about it. Which is the worst homework for him? Math? Writing? Consider that the work may be difficult or frustrating for him. There could be a good reason he is avoiding it. Maybe he feels his teacher is being mean to him.)

After spending a lot of time talking about what a misery homework can be, you can finally sigh and say, "We need some ideas. Your teacher will not be happy with no homework. We need to figure out the least painful way to get your assignments done."

Then get a pencil and paper and write down all the questions and ideas the two of you can think of. Here are some you can start with:

- Is it easier to get it done right away, or to play and eat first?
- How about starting with playing, and then sitting down to tackle the homework when I start making dinner? We could work together in the kitchen.
- Would it help to have music while you work or is quiet better?
- Would it be good to have a special snack to nibble on while working or to have a snack to look forward to when you're finished?
- How much time do you think it should take? (Some kids see homework stretching out endlessly, so a time limit is a great help to them.) How about you setting the timer yourself? If you agree to work *steadily*, homework will be done when the timer rings! (Kids often insist on finishing their work even *after* the timer rings. ["I just have a little bit more to go, Mom."] They are encouraged by their own progress.)

Include every single idea he comes up with, even if it is silly. ("Throw the homework in the fire!") After all the ideas are written down, he can choose from among the ones that are acceptable to both of you. Having your son come up with his own ideas is very different from making him promise to obey you. (Keep in mind that he may need the comfort of having his complaints about homework acknowledged long after solutions have been discussed and agreed upon: "Stupid, boring homework!")

Why is this different from just extracting a promise from him? *Because you listened to his feelings first.* You are on his side instead of on the teacher's side, against him. And because he participated in coming up with the solution, he has more motivation to make it work. You will be giving your son two gifts—some understanding and some control over his own life.

What can you do about the bickering between the children?

We have written an entire book in answer to this question, called *Siblings Without Rivalry.* One of our major recommendations is to involve the children in finding solutions to their problems rather than imposing a solution upon them. A father told us:

> My two daughters (five and eight) were fighting over who would sit in the front seat of the car next to Daddy. I said, "Cut it out, girls. Today Annie can sit up front with me and tomorrow Katie can sit there. And if you don't like that idea, here's another: Annie can sit up front on the way to the store and Katie can sit up front on the way home."
>
> They didn't like either of my suggestions (which I thought were pretty good) and kept on fighting. Suddenly I remembered to turn it over to them. I said, "Boy, this is a tough problem. But I have a lot of confidence in you two. You'll probably be able to figure out some kind of solution that feels fair to each of you."
>
> They came up with the darndest idea. Since Katie was eight (an even number) and Annie was five (an odd number), they decided to split up the days of the month

> according to odd and even. On odd days Annie (five) sits in the front. On even days Katie (eight) sits in the front. It's been working beautifully. I don't even have to remind them.

Even very young children can work out the conflicts between them. One mother wrote to tell us:

> I have a success story to report using ideas from your books with a four-year-old and a two-and-a-half-year-old.
>
> My daughter, Shari (two and a half), had invited Molly (four) to spend the afternoon with us. We were all a little cranky, and before long their play in the den became shrill and approached the "pull hair and shove" stage. It seems they both wanted to watch a different video.
>
> I was simply too drained to deal with it so I marched in and recited the "routine" like a script: "I can see that you are both really upset. Each of you wants to watch your favorite video, and it's very hard to figure out what to do. You two have been friends for a long time and I'm sure you can settle this in a way that feels good to both of you."
>
> I left the room. Within one minute Molly and Shari came into the kitchen HOLDING HANDS! "We decided to watch the end of Molly's video first and then we'll watch the beginning of Shari's video."
>
> I was so proud of them. And proud of myself, too!

How do you feel about giving children "time outs"?

Whenever we're uncertain about using a particular method with a child, we ask ourselves, "Is this a method we would like used with ourselves in our most caring relationships?" Suppose, for example, that I had carelessly made out a check on an overdrawn account, causing my husband to receive an embarrassing phone call at work from a bill collector. And further suppose that when he came home from work he said to me sternly, "That's it. I've had it. I am giving you a 'time out.' I want you to go into your room right now and think about what you did."

How would I experience his words? I'd feel as if I were being punished or excommunicated. I'd think, "I must be such an awful person that I need to be sent away." Or I might become defiant and counterattack with "I haven't noticed *you* being Mr. Perfect lately. You let the car run out of gas last week," and the fight would be on.

However, if *he* took a "time out," saying something like "I'm really upset about that bounced check and I don't want to let it out on you. I'm going to sit down with the paper a while and cool off a little," I'd probably feel contrite. Later, I'd tell him how sorry I was to have caused him the embarrassment and tell myself to make sure that it didn't happen again.

We therefore recommend to parents who are thinking of ordering a child to take a "time out" that they consider instead taking a "time out" themselves.

One mother told us she said to her two shrieking teenagers, "I am so angry my stomach is churning. I can't listen to this screaming anymore. It's a beautiful day and I'm going out for a walk now." This mother also said she thinks of "time out" as a gift she gives to herself rather than a disciplinary measure to use on her children.

One father informed us that he had progressed from spanking his kids, to using "time-outs," to expressing his strong feelings—with few words. He found that one loud, *"I don't like what I see!"* or "Children, here's what I expect . . ." usually led to improved behavior.

This next question is one that we ask of parents. We know that notes can be a powerful means of communication and so when we give workshops, our question to parents is "How do you use notes?"

Two parents told us they write notes as a way of managing their own angry feelings. Here are their stories:

> I have seven children, ages seven to eighteen—four girls and three boys. I get tired of talking and they get tired of listening. So I write them a lot of notes. One day after they left for school I checked their rooms. The girls' room was disgusting—dirty clothes, underwear, food, etc. I was furious. I took my paper and black marker and proceeded to write the girls a letter describing what I saw (a pigsty), what I thought of them (pigs), and what I expected of them when I came home (a clean room or else!). Then I pinned the letter—sheets and sheets of paper on their curtains. As the day passed I would return to the disaster area and reread my letter. Each time I would unpin the pages and rewrite my expectations and feelings on fresh paper in a more civilized form. My final letter was actually friendly. The whole process made me feel better. Putting my frustration in writing gave me a chance to explode and then to choose my words. It gave me time to change from attacking my daughters to attacking the problem.

This next example is from a single mother:

> **Situation:**
> The living room was a mess—beyond the ability of Jeremy, my six-year-old, to organize the cleanup. It was late, I was tired, and I have a tendency to get very angry when I have to repeat myself and I did not want to supervise another cleanup.
>
> **Mother's solution:**
> On a large piece of paper I listed each task by number and in a new color. I also drew a small picture:

1. Blocks

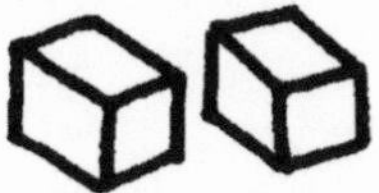

2. Figures (dolls, robots, puppets)

3. Legos

4. Crayons

5. Books

Jeremy studied my note, smiled, and went to work. Not only did he complete the job, but there were unexpected results:

1. My son's pride at having cleaned up the whole living room by himself.
2. His feeling of self-importance as he crossed off each task. ("Mom, one and three are done!")
3. His new image of himself as a "big-guy memo reader."
4. His discovery that a BIG JOB solution is made up of a lot of little jobs.

It's not likely that you'd ever think of writing a note for a child who is too young to read and yet parents who have tried this approach report success:

> My two-year-old kept forgetting to close the potty after using it. His baby brother was old enough to crawl over and splash in it, but not old enough to open the lid. I taped a note to the inside of the potty lid. It said, "Please close lid after using potty."
>
> The older one could not read, but he brought me the note, asked me to read it to him, and then taped it back on the lid. He was fascinated that I wrote to him and from then on remembered to close the potty!

I don't like using the television set as a babysitter, but when I'm preparing dinner, I don't want the kids underfoot or fighting with each other. Any suggestions?

One mother we know solved the too-much-TV problem by turning her dinner preparation time into storytime for the whole family. She told her children that she loved to listen to stories while she made dinner and asked them to bring their favorite books to the kitchen to read aloud to her and to each other while she worked. The children loved the idea. They took pride in selecting the stories they would read and listened with great appreciation to each other. The mother reported several other bonuses: the children watched less TV; they became better readers; their vocabulary improved; they fought less with each other. Best of all, the good mood continued into the dinner hour and the stories provided food for family discussion.

Is there any way to help a child cope with her fear of monsters? I've tried telling my daughter that there is no such thing as a monster, but she's still very fearful.

Over the years parents have shared with us a variety of ways to deal with monsters. Some have given their children a magic word to say that would chase the monsters away. Some have taped a note onto the bedroom door: "Monsters Keep Out!" Some buy their children a special stuffed animal, a "brave buddy," who will watch over and protect them through the night. One father concocted a "magic potion" (vinegar and toothpaste) and placed a dish of the strong smelling stuff near the open window to ward off monsters.

In the next few stories you'll read about parents who have encouraged their children to come up with their own solutions. As you read each account you'll notice that the solutions worked primarily because of the parents' acceptance of their children's perceptions and the children's participation in finding their own answers:

> My four-year-old, Jesse, had frequent night terrors. He'd scream wildly and it was impossible to calm him. Finally we asked him what he thought he needed to do to make the

monsters go away and stay away. Jesse said that maybe a wall could keep the monsters away. My husband asked if we could manage without real wood or stones. Jesse said, "Of course. We'll build an imaginary wall that only monsters can see . . . and we'll paint it brown 'cause monsters hate brown."

We spent a long time building an imaginary wall around Jesse's bed. After what felt like an hour of piling on mortar and stones Jesse said, "This is great. Now we need some ROAR so when the monsters touch the wall it will ROAR and scare them away."

Jesse ran to the pantry and came back with an empty jar. "What's that for?" we asked.

"There's ROAR in here," he said and then poured the imaginary ROAR on the imaginary wall and kept the jar by his bed so that he could "pour more of it on the spots that were leaking away ROAR."

Jesse chose the solution, participated in the experience, and as a result—the monsters moved on.

* * *

At two-and-a-half, Michael, under a lot of stress from a new baby, began to have nightmares about terrible monsters living in all of the corners of his room. After a week of trying everything with no success, I asked Michael what he thought I should do. He said, "Sweep them away." I took a broom to the corners of his room, swept the monsters into the hall and out of the door, and said, "Good-bye, don't come back!"

After a few days Michael decided that he wanted to confront the monsters. To solve the problem of broom waving by a two-year-old, I suggested the feather duster as the tool of choice. Michael agreed. For about a week he dusted the monsters out of the room, and he's never had a monster in his room since.

* * *

At about age three my son had his first nightmare and for a few nights following he was afraid to go to sleep. I lay down beside him and asked what he thought we could do to make the room feel safe. Much to my surprise he said, "Orange dust will keep it safe."

I said, "Really?"

He said, "Yes, and we'll wash out the room with colors."

Well, I know he loves to paint and draw so I asked, "How do you do that?"

He said, "Close your eyes and feel the blue color wash out your body and swirl out the floor. Then we'll pick up the green and swish it around the roof and corners and swirl it out the floor—down, down, down into the ground." He's never had a nightmare or night fear since.

Can these communication skills be used with older children?

Yes. The principles and skills in *How to Be the Parent You Always Wanted to Be* apply to people of all ages and to all caring relationships. Here are letters from three different parents who describe touching moments that took place between themselves and their teenagers:

My daughter, Betsy (thirteen), is a hypersensitive, prickly kind of "touch me not" person. It doesn't take much to make her fly off the handle. Yesterday morning I had to get to my How to Talk . . . workshop so I asked my husband to drive Betsy and the younger children to school for me. As I was gathering my things to go, I noticed that Betsy had not allowed enough time to get ready. Her father was fuming as she was fussing with her hair in front of the mirror. "You're going to make me late with all your foolishness," he yelled.

"No one is going to care how your hair looks. We've got to go NOW!!"

Betsy looked as if she were going to "lose it." I walked over to her and said, "It's an awful feeling to be rushed—especially when you want to look nice." Well, this child who shuns any physical expression of caring, turned to me, gave me a big bear hug, and ran out the door.

* * *

There was a bad winter storm and we had a townwide blackout. It was predicted that the power outage would last for more than a week. Since my ninety-year-old mother was living with us, and I didn't want her to get chilled, I booked a hotel for our family. When I told my fifteen-year-old daughter we had to pack, she threw a fit.

"It's not fair. . . . I don't want to go to a hotel. . . . You can't make me. . . . School is closed and all my friends are going to hang out together. . . . You're ruining it!"

She flounced off to sulk on her bed.

A thousand things to say to her ran through my head:

"How can you be so selfish? Do you want your grandmother to get sick? Why don't you take this opportunity to spend some quality time with her? She might not even be alive this time next year. Your friends are not going to be hanging out with no electricity. That means no TV, no computers, no showers, no opening the refrigerator every five minutes. Do you realize people are actually suffering in this storm? It's not all about you!"

After allowing myself the satisfaction of all these thoughts, I was able to go into her room and say sincerely, "I can see how disappointing this is for you. You were really looking forward to staying here and hanging out with your friends." Then I left the room.

Five minutes later she came into the kitchen and cheerfully helped us pack. It was like I had waved a magic wand.

* * *

Jaimie, my sixteen-year-old daughter, had a Spanish composition due Monday morning. She had been stewing about it all weekend as she often feels that writing is not her strength. It was Sunday night and I had had a busy day with dinner, chores, paying bills, etc., and had settled down in front of the TV to watch a movie. Finally, some rest and relaxation, peace and quiet . . . until Jaimie storms into the room, drops her books on the floor, sighs heavily, and begins to write. Out of the corner of my eye I note her agitation.

JAIMIE: This is so stupid! The Spanish teacher is such a jerk.

I'm beginning to get annoyed. I'm tempted to say something like, "You knew you had this assignment. Why did you wait till the last minute? Stop complaining. You're interfering with my relaxation, etc."

Jaimie would probably have screamed that I didn't understand her or that I never listened. She would have burst out crying, stormed out of the room, angry at me, and I would be furious with her.

Luckily the red flag went up in my brain: Teenager in distress! So instead here's what happened:

ME: Sounds like this assignment isn't easy.

JAIMIE: Yeah (*eyes brimming with tears*). She's so stupid.

ME: You feel your Spanish teacher was unfair in giving the class this assignment?

JAIMIE: No . . . it's just that I thought this class would be more conversational Spanish.

ME: Oh, so you thought you would be speaking, not writing.

JAIMIE: (*eyes not as teary*) Yeah. (*She is writing furiously.*)

Finally she closed her notebook.

ME: So you finished! That must feel good.
JAIMIE: (*big sigh of relief*) Yeah!
ME: What was your topic?
JAIMIE: I had to write about the person I admire most.
ME: Oh, who did you write about?
JAIMIE: You.

For More Information

If you'd like to learn more about how to communicate helpfully with your children, you can choose from among the books by Adele Faber and Elaine Mazlish listed on page 3 of this book.

A good starting point would be: *How to Talk So Kids Will Listen & Listen So Kids Will Talk.*

If you're interested in getting together with other parents to discuss and practice the skills in this and other books by the authors, you can request information about their group workshop programs. For further details, please visit their website, www.fabermazlish.com, or contact them directly.

info@fabermazlish.com

1-800-944-8584

Faber/Mazlish Workshops
P.O. Box 1072
Carmel, NY 10512

Index

Index

Index

John Mazlish

Adele Faber

John Mazlish

Elaine Mazlish

Internationally acclaimed experts on communication between adults and children, Adele Faber and Elaine Mazlish have won the gratitude of parents and the enthusiastic endorsement of the professional community.

Their first book, *Liberated Parents/Liberated Children*, received the Christopher Award for "literary achievement affirming the highest values of the human spirit." Their subsequent books, *How to Talk So Kids Will Listen & Listen So Kids Will Talk* and the #1 *New York Times* bestseller *Siblings Without Rivalry*, have sold more than four million copies and have been translated into over thirty languages. *How to Talk So Kids Can Learn: At Home and in School* was cited by *Child* magazine as the "best book of the year for excellence in family issues in education." The authors' group workshop programs and videos are currently being used by thousands of parent and teacher groups worldwide to improve relationships with children. Their most recent book, *How to Talk So Teens Will Listen & Listen So Teens Will Talk*, tackles the tough problems of the teenage years.

Both authors studied with the late child psychologist Dr. Haim Ginott and are former members of the faculty of the New School for Social Research in New York and the Family Life Institute of Long Island University. In addition to their frequent lectures throughout the United States, Canada, and abroad, they have appeared on every major television talk show from *Oprah* to *Good Morning America*. They currently reside in Long Island, New York, and each is the parent of three children.